TEDDY BEAR
MATH

Barbara Barbieri McGrath
Illustrated by **Tim Nihoff**

Charlesbridge

Published by Charlesbridge
85 Main Street
Watertown, MA 02472
(617) 926-0329
www.charlesbridge.com

Library of Congress Cataloging-in-Publication Data
McGrath, Barbara Barbieri, 1954–
    Teddy bear math / Barbara Barbieri McGrath;
illustrated by Tim Nihoff.
       p. cm.
    ISBN 978-1-58089-283-4 (reinforced for library use)
    ISBN 978-1-58089-284-1 (softcover)
1. Mathematics—Juvenile literature. I. Nihoff, Tim. II. Title.
QA40.5.M42 2011
510—dc22   2010023548

Printed in China
(hc) 10 9 8 7 6 5 4 3 2 1
(sc) 10 9 8 7 6 5 4 3 2 1

Illustrations hand drawn digitally in Adobe Photoshop
Display type set in Animated Gothic and
    text type set in Century Schoolbook
Color separations by Chroma Graphics, Singapore
Manufactured by Regent Publishing Services, Hong Kong
Printed February 2011 in Shenzhen, Guangdong, China
Production supervision by Brian G. Walker
Designed by Susan Mallory Sherman

A bear hug to Brody! Love, B. B. M.

To the loving memory of my mom, from
her number three, who called me her
little Timmer Teddy Bear. XO—T. N.

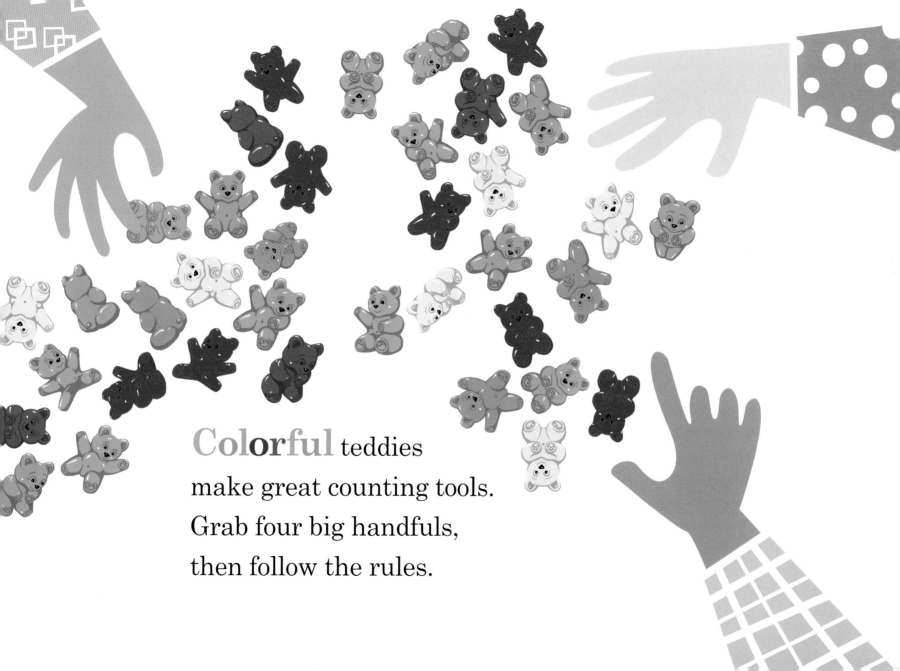

Colorful teddies
make great counting tools.
Grab four big handfuls,
then follow the rules.

Take a quick glance—
you don't need to count.
Keep a guess in your head
of the total amount.

40?

Sort the teddies by colors.
How many sets did you get?
We'll use them in groups,
so don't move them just yet.

Let's make a graph
where the bears climb and play.
For solving math problems
a graph is the way!

In the row that reads "red,"
place the reds from your pile.
Put a red bear in each box—
this might take a while.

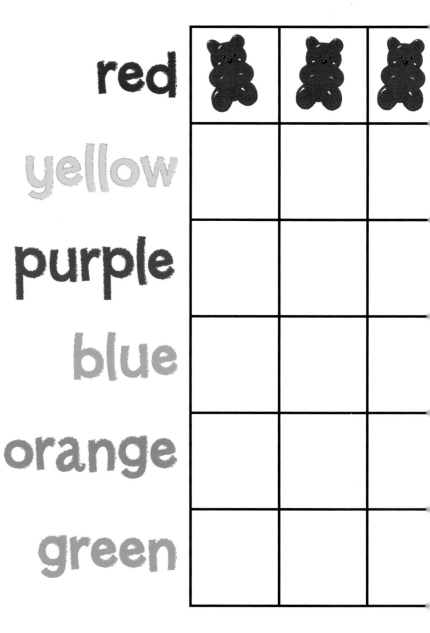

Now do the same
with yellow, purple, and blue.
Don't forget orange
and green teddies, too.

Examine the bears
when your hard work has ceased.
Which row has the most?
Which row has the least?

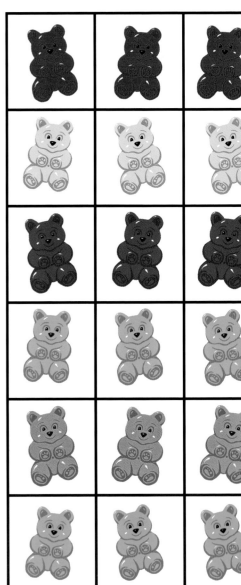

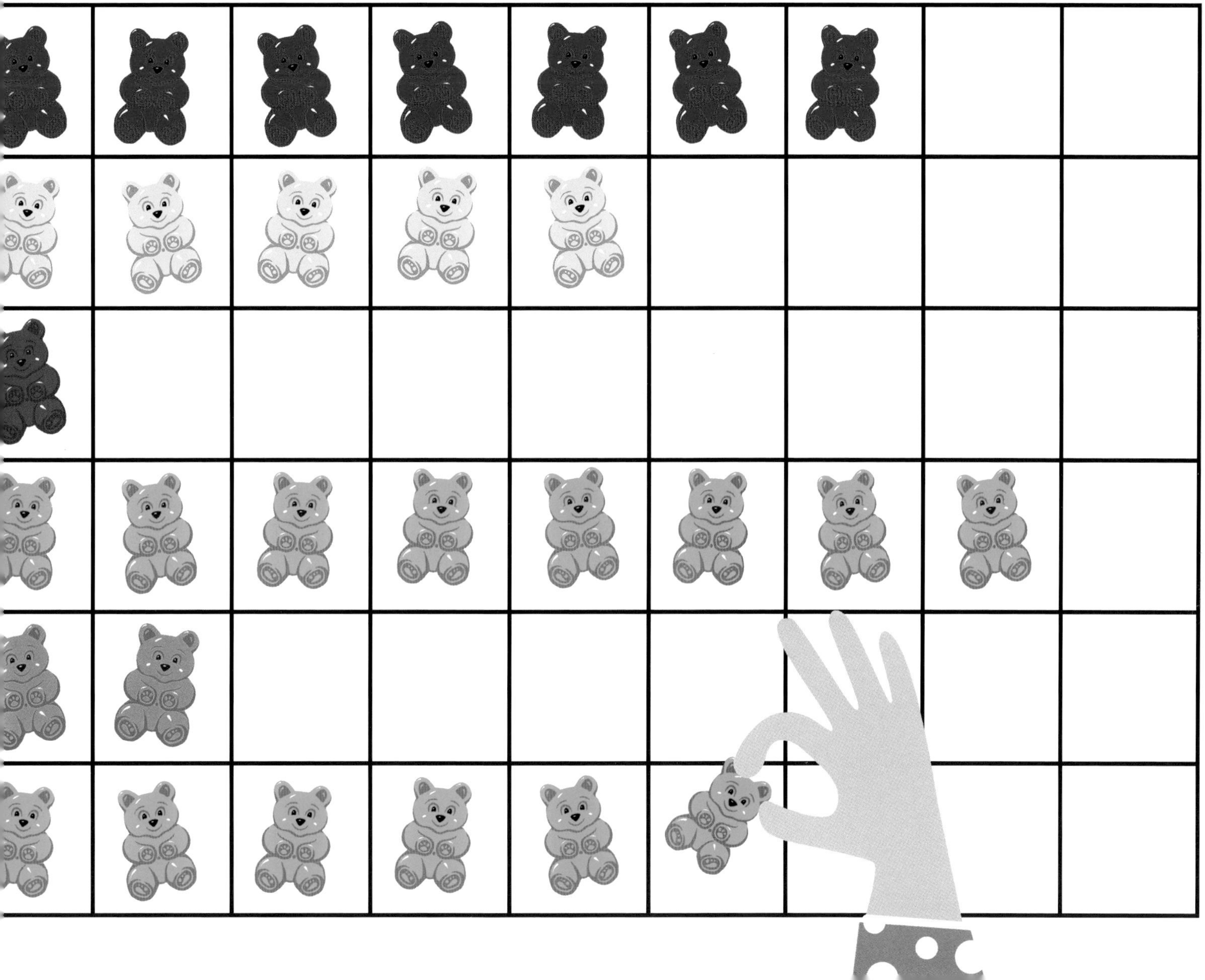

Short, long, or equal?
Compare the six rows.
The more bears you add,
the longer each grows.

Write down the total
you see in each row.
Let's see if your guess
was too high or too low.

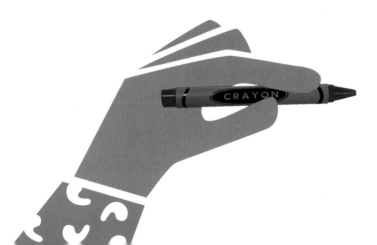

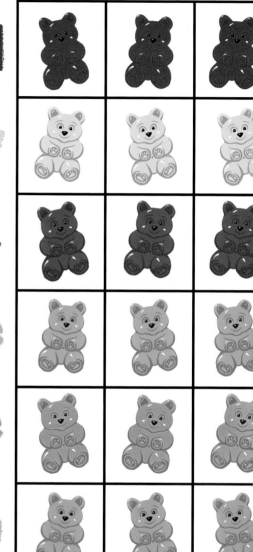

red

yellow

purple

blue

orange

green

🐻	🐻	🐻	🐻	🐻	🐻	🐻		**10**
🐻	🐻	🐻	🐻	🐻				8
🐻								**4**
🐻	🐻	🐻	🐻	🐻	🐻	🐻	🐻	11
🐻	🐻							5
🐻	🐻	🐻	🐻	🐻	🐻			9

Now add them together.
The sum will be grand.
You can add all the numbers
or count each bear by hand.

Color	Count
red	10
yellow	8
purple	4
blue	11
orange	5
green	9

```
  2
 10
  8
  4
 11
  5
+ 9
────
 47
```

Was the number you reached
more or less than you thought?
Take the small from the large.
That's the difference you've got.

```
  47
- 40
────
   7
```

The teddies are waiting
to try something new.
With math there is always
a new thing to do.

It's time now to multiply—
and time to divide!
Push the teddies together.
Use these words as a guide.

It's easy to divide
the teddies by two.
Let's do it like this:
one for me, one for you!

Are the amounts unequal,
or are they the same?
You'll find in division
one bear can "remain."

$$2\sqrt{\overline{47}} = 23\text{r}1$$

$$\begin{array}{r} 23\text{r}1 \\ 2\overline{)47} \\ 4 \\ \hline 07 \\ 6 \\ \hline 1 \end{array}$$

If you have a remainder,
move that bear to the side.
What happens next?
Something bears haven't tried.

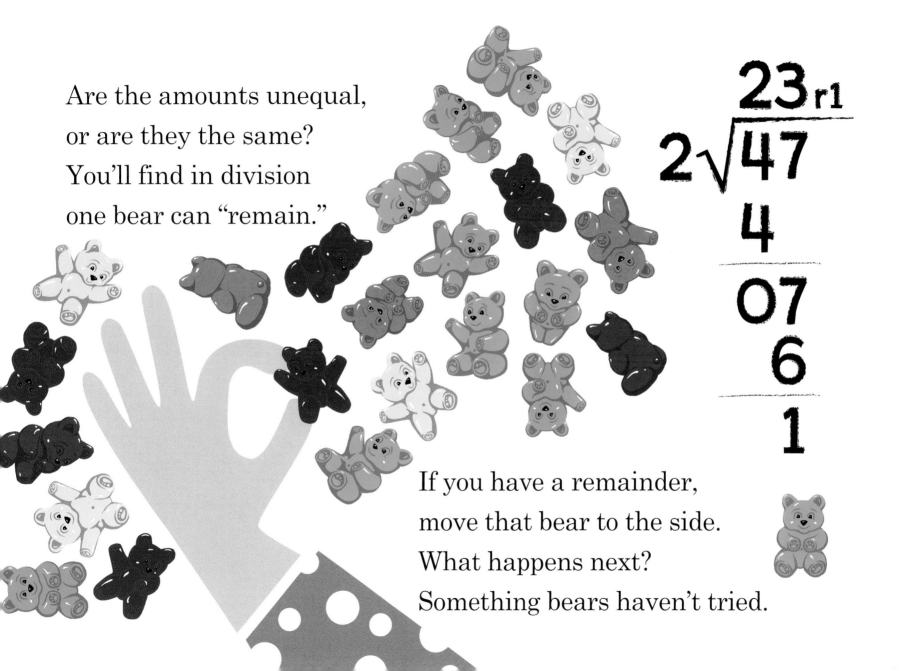

Split the two bunches
so the teddies can make
four groups of ten bears—
all the rest take a break.

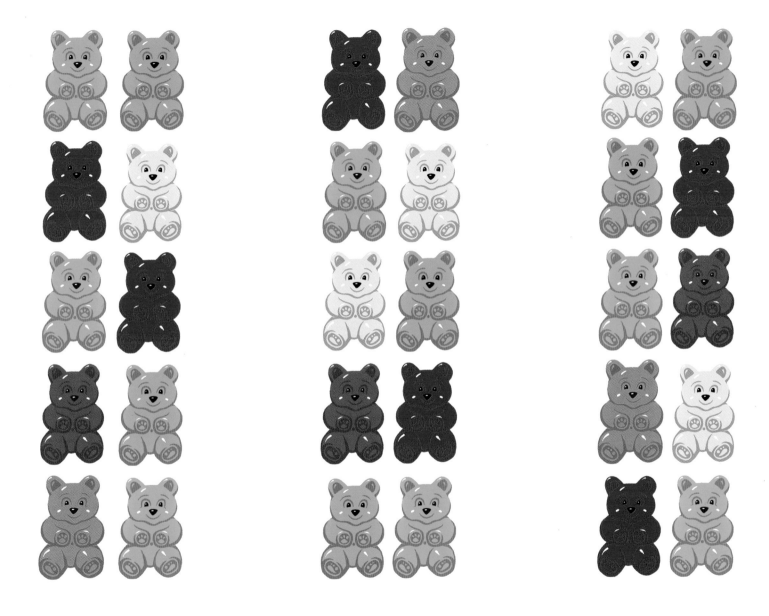

Multiply the bears!

Do this carefully.

Four times ten is forty,

as you now can see.

4 x 10 = 40

It's time to arrange
the four groups into eight.
Five bears in each group
means you're doing just great.

Count by fives up to forty.

The total is clear.

What's eight times five bears?

The answer's right here.

8 x 5 = 40

Multiplying numbers
is a fun thing to do.
Next use the bears
to find ten teddies times two.

$$10 \times 2 = 20$$

If you turn it around,
will you see twenty again?
Yes! That's the product
of two bears times ten.

$$2 \times 10 = 20$$

You have solved much,
and you have learned plenty.
But do you know
how many fives make up twenty?

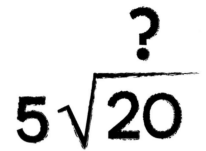

On the subject of twenty,
bears can do more.
You'll get the same number
with five groups of four.

5 x 4 = 20

Take one bear of each color.
Put them all in a line.
Start with your favorite—
six bears look just fine!

It's time now to say
good-bye to the rest.
They love doing math
and think you're the best!

For the six that are left
slowly follow each word:
the fourth bear goes first,
the fifth second, the third third!

3rd 1st 2nd

The second goes fourth.
He trots away fast.
The sixth will be fifth,
and the first will be last.

6th 4th 3rd 1st 2nd 5th

Congratulations! Great job!
You're on the right path.
You followed directions
and did teddy bear math!

Here's a review so that you can look
at all of the math you learned in this book.

GRAPHING

1. Sort the bears by color.
2. Compare rows with the most and least.
3. Find equal rows.
4. Find the number of bears in each row.
5. Add the numbers or count the bears to find the total amount.

ADDITION AND SUBTRACTION

$$\begin{array}{r} \overset{2}{1}0 \\ 8 \\ 4 \\ 11 \\ 5 \\ +\ 9 \\ \hline 47 \end{array} \qquad \begin{array}{r} 47 \\ -40 \\ \hline 7 \end{array}$$

MULTIPLICATION

$10 \times 2 = 20$

is the same as

$2 \times 10 = 20$

DIVISION

$$2\overline{)47}\ \ {}^{23\text{r}1}$$
$$\begin{array}{r} 4 \\ \hline 07 \\ 6 \\ \hline 1 \end{array}$$

ORDINAL NUMBERS

1st 2nd 3rd 4th 5th 6th